WHAT'S INSIDE A DVD Player?

ARNOLD RINGSTAD

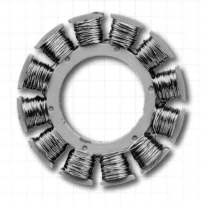

Published by The Child's World®
1980 Lookout Drive • Mankato, MN 56003-1705
800-599-READ • www.childsworld.com

Photographs ©: Rick Orndorf, cover (DVD player), cover (jacks), 1 (DVD player), 1 (jacks),
4, 6, 7, 11, 13 (tray), 14, 15 (motors), 17, 18, 19, 20 (jacks), 24; JV Korotkova/Shutterstock
Images, cover (laser head), 1 (laser head), 9 (laser head), 15 (laser head), 20 (laser head);
Shutterstock Images, 2, 3 (circuit board), 3 (plug), 5 (glasses), 5 (scissors), 8, 9 (DVD), 12,
13 (screws) 16, 21, 22, 23 (screws); Praiwun Thungsarn/Shutterstock, 3 (screwdriver), 5
(screwdriver), 10, 23 (screwdriver); Shyripa Alexandr/Shutterstock Images, 5 (gloves)

ISBN 9781503832046
LCCN 2018962807

Printed in the United States of America
PA02419

About the Author

Arnold Ringstad lives in Minnesota. He likes
to watch old TV shows with his DVD player.

Contents

Materials and Safety

Materials

- ☐ DVD player
- ☐ Phillips screwdriver
- ☐ Safety glasses
- ☐ Scissors
- ☐ Work gloves

Safety

- Always be careful with sharp objects like screwdrivers.

- Unplug the DVD player, and then cut its power cord before you start. Throw the end of the power cord away.

- Wear work gloves to protect your hands from sharp edges.

- Wear safety glasses in case pieces snap off.

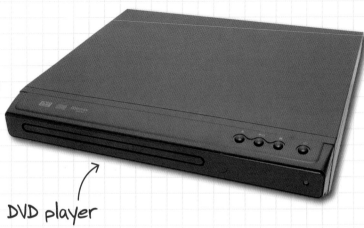

DVD player

Important!

Be sure to get an adult's permission before taking anything apart. When you're taking things apart, have an adult nearby in case you need help or have questions.

Phillips screwdriver

Work gloves

Scissors

Safety glasses

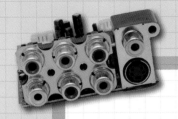

Inside a DVD Player

People use DVD players to watch movies. The movies come on discs. The discs are called DVDs. *DVD* stands for digital **versatile** disc. The DVD player reads information off the disc. Then it sends that information to a TV. How does a DVD player work? What's inside?

Cover

Audio/video jacks

Power cord

Laser

Base

Disc tray

Circuit boards

Button switches

DVDs

A DVD has a long, spiraling pattern of tiny pits. They are too small for the eye to see. If you stretched the pattern into a straight line, it would be more than 7 miles (11 km) long! The pits and the gaps between them represent information. They make up the pictures and sounds of a movie.

DVDs store a lot of information in a flat disc.

Opening the DVD Player

First, unplug the DVD player and cut the power cord for safety. Then, look at the base of the player. Screws hold it together. Use a screwdriver to remove them. There may be more screws on the back. Remove all of these screws, too.

Safety Note

Be sure the DVD player is unplugged before you cut the power cord.

Safety Note
Be careful not to
lose the screws.

Now the cover will come off. Take
a look at what's inside.

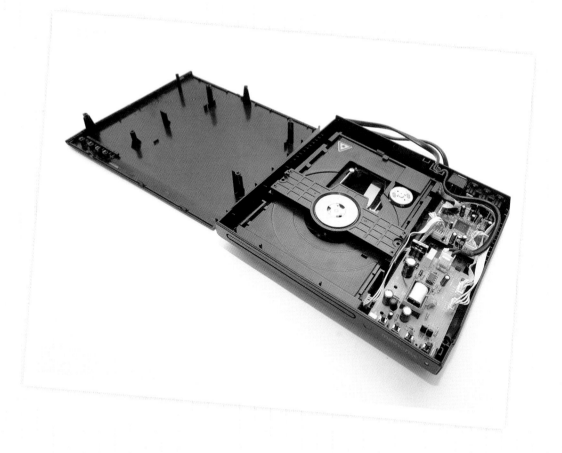

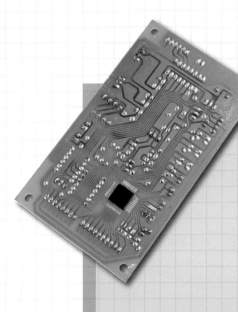

Removing the Parts

Plastic clips hold some of the parts in place. There may be more screws, too. Undo the clips and remove the screws. Then you can take the parts out from the base. The parts you will see are the **circuit boards** and the disc tray.

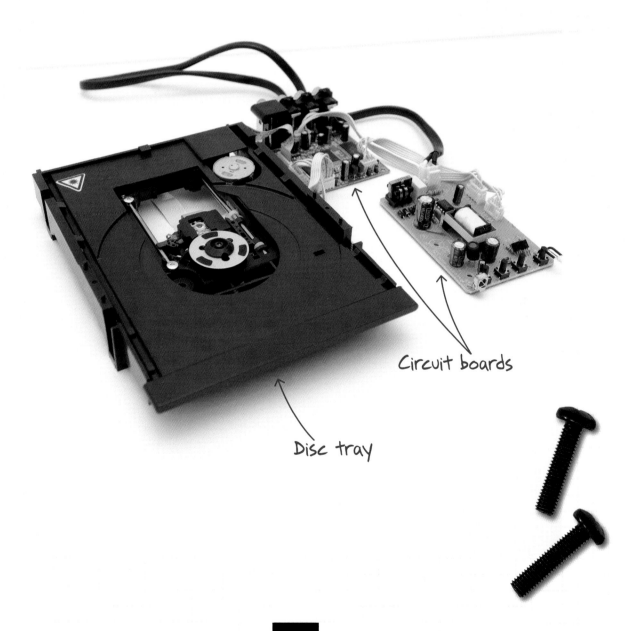

Circuit boards

Disc tray

The Disc Tray

The disc tray has a **laser** in it. The laser points upward at the spinning DVD. The laser reflects differently off the pits and gaps. A **sensor** detects the reflections.

Laser

Motors

Then it sends this information to the circuit boards.

The disc tray has three **motors**. The first pushes the tray in and out. The second spins the disc around. The third moves the laser back and forth.

Circuit Boards

The circuit boards are the brains
of the DVD player. They receive
information about the pits and
gaps. They turn that pattern into
video and sound.

Safety Note

Circuit boards may have sharp edges.
Be careful when handling them.

Front and Back

The circuit board in front has
switches on it. This is where
the DVD player's buttons are.
Another circuit board is in the back.

Front
circuit board

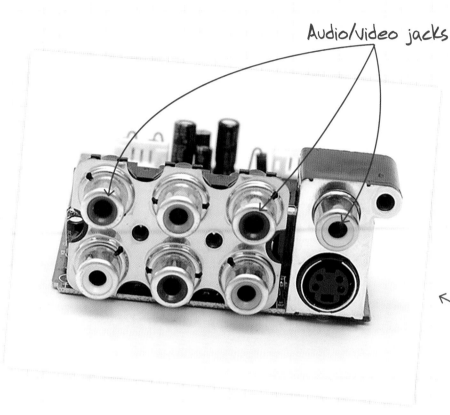

Audio/video jacks

Rear
circuit board

It has the audio/video **jacks**. They
carry the video and sound signals
to a TV. The power cord also enters
the player here. It provides the
electricity the player needs to work.

Reusing a DVD Player

We've taken apart a DVD player and learned what's inside. Now what? Here are some ideas for how to reuse the parts of a DVD player. Can you think of any more?

- **Carrying Case:** Take out the DVD player's parts, then put the top back on. Now you can use the empty shell to store things.

- **Wall Art:** Remove a circuit board. Find a small piece of wood to use as backing. Then, use screws to attach the circuit board to the wood. Hang it up as artwork!

Glossary

circuit board (SUR-kit BORD): A circuit board is a piece of material that holds computer chips, switches, and other parts. Inside the DVD player, a circuit board turns a pattern of information into video and sound.

jacks (JAKS): Jacks are places where cords can plug in to send or receive signals. Cords plugged into jacks carry video and sound between the DVD player and television.

laser (LAY-zur): A laser is a very focused beam of light. A laser shines on the spinning DVD to help read the information on the disc.

motor (MOH-tur): A motor is a part of a machine that creates motion. A motor in the disc tray spins the DVD at high speed.

sensor (SEN-sur): A sensor is a part of a machine that detects or measures something. A sensor in a DVD player detects the laser's reflections.

versatile (VUR-suh-tuhl): Something that's versatile can be used for many things. DVDs are versatile because they can be used for movies, music, and more.

To Learn More

IN THE LIBRARY

Holzweiss, Kristina. *Amazing Makerspace DIY Basic Machines*. New York, NY: Scholastic, 2018.

Kenney, Karen Latchana. *Who Invented the Television? Sarnoff vs. Farnsworth*. Minneapolis, MN: Lerner Publishing Group, 2018.

Laine, Carolee. *Inventing the Television*. Mankato, MN: The Child's World, 2016.

ON THE WEB

Visit our website for links about taking apart a DVD player: **childsworld.com/links**

Note to Parents, Teachers, and Librarians: We routinely verify our Web links to make sure they are safe and active sites. So encourage your readers to check them out!

Index